Discard

The Wild Girl

For Mary, Jane, and Jo

Copyright © Chris Wormell, 2005
The right of Chris Wormell to be identified as the author of this work has been asserted in accordance with the Copyright, Designs and Patents Act 1988.

Published in Great Britain by Jonathan Cape, an imprint of Random House Children's Books, in 2005

This edition published 2006 by Eerdmans Books for Young Readers, an imprint of William B. Eerdmans Publishing Company
255 Jefferson SE, Grand Rapids, Michigan 49503
P.O. Box 163, Cambridge CB3 9PU U.K.
www.eerdmans.com/youngreaders

ISBN-10: 0-8028-5311-0 / ISBN-13: 978-0-8028-5311-0 (alk.paper)

06 07 08 09 10 6 5 4 3 2 1

Library of Congress Cataloging-in-Publication Data
Wormell, Christopher.
The wild girl / Chris Wormell.
p. cm.
Summary: A young girl and a little brown dog live together, alone in the wilderness, until a big bear tries to share their cave.
[1. Feral children--Fiction. 2. Dogs--Fiction. 3. Bears--Fiction.] I. Title.
PZ7.W88773Wi 2006
[E]--dc22
2005033657

Printed in Singapore

The Wild Girl

Chris Wormell

EERDMANS BOOKS FOR YOUNG READERS

GRAND RAPIDS, MICHIGAN • CAMBRIDGE, U.K.

This is the story of a little girl and a small brown dog who lived all alone in the wilderness. The little girl had no one to brush her hair, or wash her face, or tie her shoelaces like you do. So her hair was a terrible mess and her face quite grubby. She had no shoelaces to tie because she had no shoes — but her feet had tough soles that were quite used to stepping on sharp stones, so she didn't need them.

The small brown dog had fleas, and I expect the little girl did too.

The little girl never went to school, because of course there
were no schools in the wilderness. She had to learn things
for herself. The small brown dog learned too.

There were no stores,
so they couldn't buy food.
They had to hunt for it.

Sometimes they
caught trout . . .

. . . and cooked them over a little fire of twigs.

Sometimes they gathered
berries and roots.

They even ate insects.

They lived in a cave
high up on the side of a
mountain. From there they
could look out and see far,
far away, almost to the edge
of the world. And in all the
wide wilderness, the little girl
never once saw the smoke
of another fire curling up
into the sky.

Sometimes she called out,
but never heard a reply, save for the
echo of her own voice, calling back
from the far mountaintops.

When the small brown dog barked,
he was puzzled — there seemed to be
lots of other dogs all around the mountains,
but he could never see any of them.

On warm summer nights, the little girl and the
small brown dog slept out under the stars.

Then, in the autumn, they gathered dry bracken and made a big nest at the back of the cave. It was cozy and snug, and mostly it was warm.

But in the coldest weather they often kept a fire burning through the night.

One winter day, the little girl and the
small brown dog were collecting firewood,
when they came upon tracks in the snow.
Big tracks.
Bear tracks.
Tracks heading towards the cave.

They followed the tracks,
and when they reached the
cave the small brown dog
began to growl.

But the bear had gone.

Inside, they found the bracken nest was squashed flat.

The small brown dog began to growl again.

He could smell bear.

They were certain the bear would come back.

And it did . . .

That night there was a
blizzard. The wind howled
and the snow began to pile
up in drifts outside the cave.
And as the little girl and the small
brown dog watched the storm, they
saw a great, dark shape coming up the
mountainside.

Soon the shape filled the mouth
of the cave . . .

The bear would have come right in, but the little girl and the small brown dog barred the way. This was their cave, and no one could take it from them — not even a big bad bear. They would fight for it!

The bear could easily have brushed them aside with a paw, but it didn't. It looked down at them with strange, sad eyes, then turned and left the cave.

The small brown dog barked, and the little girl cried out in triumph
and threw a snowball after the bad old bear as it disappeared
into the stormy night.

Then they heard a
sound from the
cave behind
them . . .

. . . and creeping out from the
darkest corner, behind the
squashed bracken nest,
came a tiny bear cub.

The little girl realized that the bear was not a bad
bear after all, just a mother bear looking for her cub.

She dropped her spear and ran out into the blizzard,
calling after the mother bear.

But she was gone, and the falling snow
had covered her tracks.

After a while, it stopped snowing. The wind broke up the clouds and the moon shone down on the wide, lonely wilderness.

There was no sign of the mother bear.

The little girl turned and trudged back up to the cave.

The snow had drifted deep, too deep for short legs,
and she carried the small brown dog under one arm
and the tiny cub under the other.

And who should they find sitting waiting
by the cave but the mother bear.

That winter, the cave high up on the mountainside was the snuggest, warmest place in all the wide wilderness.

But by the spring, they all had fleas!

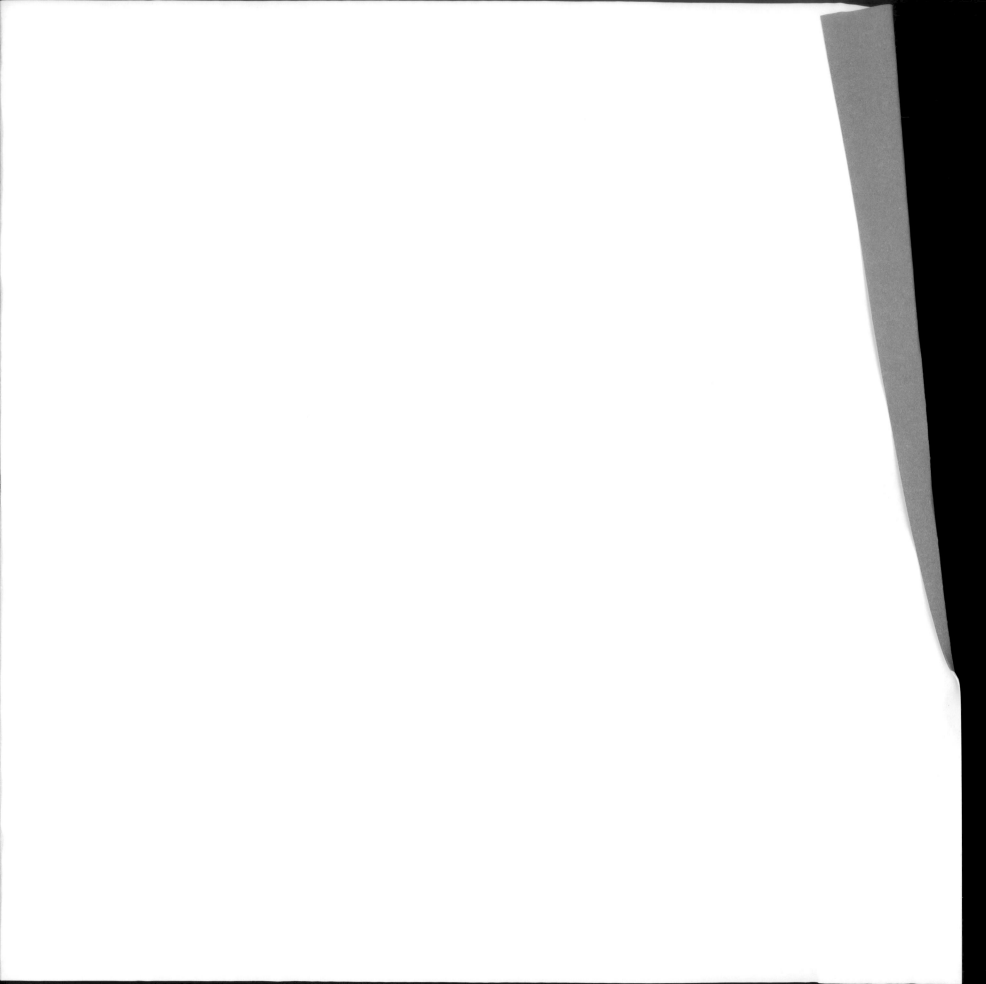